Welcome to The Castle of Mey

Her Majesty Queen Elizabeth The Queen Mother first saw what was then Barrogill Castle in 1952, while mourning the death of her husband, King George VI.

Falling for its ruined isolated charm, and hearing it was to be abandoned, she declared:
"Never! It's part of Scotland's heritage. *I'll* save it."

THE CASTLE & GARDENS OF MEY

Having acquired the most northerly castle on the British mainland, she renovated and restored it and created the beautiful gardens you see today. For almost half a century she spent many happy summers here and shorter visits at other times of the year.

The warmth and affection of the people of Caithness combined with the county's great beauty, meant that The Queen Mother always enjoyed staying at the Castle of Mey.

We hope that you too will enjoy the Castle's unique atmosphere.

THE QUEEN ELIZABETH CASTLE OF MEY TRUST
President - HRH The Prince Charles, Duke of Rothesay

HM Queen Elizabeth The Queen Mother at The Castle of Mey in October 1955, with one of her corgis, Honey.

Photos: Nick McCann

"Caithness is a county of such great beauty, combining as it does the peace and tranquility of an open and uncrowded countryside with the rugged glory of a magnificent coastline.

It is a delight to me now that I have a home here."

HISTORY

'Flank'd with the Marine coast, prospective stands,
Right opposite the Orcade Iles and Lands;
Where I for floures, ingorg'd strong wines of Spain,
And liquored French, both Red and White amaine;
Which Palace doth contain, two four-squared courts
Graft with brave words, where the Art-drawn pensile sports,
On Hall, high Chambers, Galleries, Office Bowres
Cells, Rooms and Turrets, Platforms, Stately Towres.'

WILLIAM LITHGOW, traveller,
after being entertained at the Castle by Sir William Sinclair
during the winter of 1629

In 1814, the artist William Daniell began his ambitious *Voyage Around Britain* in Caithness. This aquatint is the earliest known image of the Castle.

The lands of Caithness were originally held by Jarls or Norse Earls. From 870 AD onwards they formed part of the Earldom of Orkney and Caithness. The land of Canisbay, on which the Castle stands, is first mentioned in the *Letters of Mey* in 1508. It is thought to have been built between 1566 and 1572 after George, 4th Earl of Caithness, acquired the Barony of Mey from the Bishop of Caithness.

The Castle's 'Z-plan' design, tower and corbelled turrets are typical of the late-16th century, as are the numerous gun slits throughout the ground and first floors and in the angles of the tower.

In 1572 the 4th Earl granted the lands to his second son, William, who became the 1st Laird of Mey. After only a year he was brutally murdered by his elder brother who was being held prisoner by their father at Girnigoe Castle near Wick. The title and Castle then passed to their brother, George, who founded the Sinclairs of Mey. Ownership of the Castle remained in the hands of the Sinclair family until the 15th Earl of Caithness died without issue in 1889. He bequeathed the Castle and its estates to his great friend P.G. Heathcote and it was later bought from Mr Heathcote's widow by Captain Imbert-Terry. On the 15th Earl's death the title passed to a relation descended from Sir James Sinclair of Mey, who had been created 1st Baronet in 1631. Malcolm, the present 20th Earl of Caithness, is a direct desendant. In 1996 it gave The Queen Mother great satisfaction to appoint the 20th Earl as one of the Trustees of The Queen Elizabeth Castle of Mey Trust, thereby re-establishing the Sinclair family's historical link with the Castle of Mey.

James Sinclair, 12th Earl of Caithness, and Postmaster General of Scotland from 1810. He was responsible for the addition of the front hall, designed by architect William Burn in 1819. He was born in the Castle, as was his son, the 13th Earl, who is referred to on the map of the estates (below right), which can be seen in the Library.

James Sinclair, 14th Earl of Caithness, inherited the title in 1855 on the death of his father. He was Vice-Admiral of Caithness and a Lord-in-Waiting to Queen Victoria. In 1866 he was created Baron Barrogill, taking the Barony's name from the Castle. A great Caithness character, he was responsible for bringing the first steam-driven car to the county in the 1870s. Less eccentric achievements included the opening of many of the county's flagstone quarries, thereby creating employment for the local community.

The next chapter of this story begins on 16th June 1952, when The Queen Mother stepped from a Viking aircraft of the King's Flight at Wick Airport and set foot in Caithness for the first time. There to greet her were her friends from the *House of the Northern Gate*, Commander and Lady Doris Vyner. On the 30-mile journey from the airport to Dunnet, she saw Barrogill Castle. "It's been up for sale for months," commented Lady Doris as the car stopped. "Do you think it would suit me?" asked The Queen Mother. Her hostess was not sure. The exterior retained a windswept romantic charm and was largely intact, but the interior was in a very poor state, having been used as a billet for Coastal Defence troops during WWII. Undeterred, Her Majesty returned a few days later to look round. There were no bathrooms, the owners, Captain and Mrs Imbert-Terry, used hip-baths, neither was there electricity, lighting being in the form of oil lamps and candles. Heat from the massive open peat fires escaped through gaping holes in the roof!

In spite of the forbidding obstacles ahead, in August 1952 the Castle became the only

property The Queen Mother ever actually owned. However, there was one thing she didn't like about her new purchase - the name. As a result, Barrogill Castle reverted to its ancient title, *the Castle of Mey*.

Now began the process of restoration and conversion from near-derelict castle to a welcoming and comfortable home. Along the way, The Queen Mother added various embellishments to the exterior such as the stone cypher above the dining room window, the entrance lanterns and the 18th-century cannons she retrieved from the waters of the Pentland Firth. These had originally been sited in a nearby battery to ward off a possible Napoleonic invasion.

In June 1996 Her Majesty formed The Queen Elizabeth Castle of Mey Trust and endowed it with the Castle, farm and estate in order to secure their future.

Copyright: RCAHMS

THE QUEEN MOTHER IN CAITHNESS

We're proud today,
For the beloved Queen Mother comes here to stay,
Not alone a Royal smile passing this way –
But coming to rest in her Castle of Mey.

So there shall be
A hundred thousand welcomes o'er land and sea,
The greeting of the Celts, its ancient heraldry,
For a Queen who has served right loyally.

Lest any dare,
To say this land is bleak or bare –
Pray have a care, yea have a care,
For the eyes of a Queen have rested there –
And behold the land is forever fair.

"CAITHNESS MAKES HER CURTSEY"
- read by the Provost of Wick, Miss Bessie Leith,
after The Queen Mother had received the Freedom of Wick in 1956.

1947. The Highland Show, Inverness. King George VI and Queen Elizabeth accompanied by Princess Margaret (partly seen) with Sir Donald Cameron of Lochiel (centre), who was appointed Lord Lieutenant of Inverness in 1939.

1952. *The House of the Northern Gate*, Dunnet Head, home of Commander and Lady Doris Vyner. The Queen Mother stayed here on numerous occasions before taking up residence in the Castle of Mey. This photograph was taken after the house was converted into a residential hotel in the early 1970s.

12th August 1955. Visiting the Castle of Mey for the first time, The Queen disembarks from the Royal Yacht *Britannia* at Dunnet Bay. She is accompanied by The Queen Mother, Princess Anne, Prince Charles, Princess Margaret and The Princess Royal. The Royal party was on its way to Balmoral at the start of the summer holidays.

Later that day eight small yachts of the Pentland Firth Yacht Club escorted the Royal Barge back to the Royal Yacht. That night *Britannia* passed Dunnet Head with her escort ship, *HMS Orwell*. The Castle of Mey was beautifully floodlit and as *Britannia* sailed past The Queen Mother's home, flares were lit at the base of the Castle walls, and rockets and parachute flares were fired from the deck of the Royal Yacht.

Saturday 11th August 1956. The Queen Mother is presented with the Freedom of Wick and becomes the first woman ever to receive the honour. She described it as "a symbol of the kindness which I have always found awaiting me in Caithness. When I came here I felt at home and among friends".

Despite the rain, huge crowds turned out at the riverside where Her Majesty inspected a Guard of Honour of the Seaforth Highlanders.

August 1964. The Queen Mother being photographed by John Adams at the Mey Sheep Dog Trials, taken by his daughter Shona. The Castle's turrets can be seen beyond the trees, on the right of the picture.

The majority of the black and white photographs in this guidebook were taken by John Adams. After vital work for the RAF Photographic Section before, during and after WWII, he set up a studio in Wick. With his friend David Oag, then Editor of the *John O'Groat Journal*, his pictures throughout 20 years helped keep Caithness in the national news.

John Adams' greatest honour was to be asked by The Queen Mother to take photographs at the Castle of Mey.

LATER YEARS

Clockwise:

1968 - Opening the Wick Central Hospital

1977 - Dancing with Major Alan Ferrier at the Royal Jubilee Ball, Wick

1990 - With the Thurso Pipe Band during Her 'Freedom of Caithness' tour

2001 - Arrival at Wick Airport in August

THIS BENCH HAS BEEN PLACED
HERE IN MEMORY OF
HER MAJESTY
QUEEN ELIZABETH
THE QUEEN MOTHER
BY HER MAJESTY'S FRIENDS,
TRUSTEES AND EMPLOYEES
AT MEY

QUEEN ELIZABETH LOVED THIS
CASTLE, WHICH SHE SAVED FROM
RUIN IN 1952, SPENDING MANY
HAPPY HOLIDAYS HERE BETWEEN
OCTOBER 1955 AND OCTOBER 2001

Opposite:
Carved from Caithness slate and unveiled in August 2002 by The Prince of Wales, the Memorial Bench faces the Pentland Firth and the Orkneys.

CASTLE TOUR

The Castle of Mey from the north east, by Tyall MacInnes.

FRONT HALL

LIBRARY

EQUERRY'S ROOM

DRAWING ROOM

DINING ROOM

BUTLER'S PANTRY & KITCHEN

GARDENS

The Queen Mother's standard incorporates the Royal Coat of Arms with that of her family, the Bowes Lyons.

FRONT HALL

Designed by architect William Burn in 1819, the front hall was added by the 12th Earl of Caithness. His portrait hangs here with those of other members of the Sinclair family.

Once The Queen Mother's interior renovation works were under way, she consulted a London firm about decoration and curtains. However, the majority of the Castle's furnishings were eventually purchased locally. Much of what you see was acquired in Thurso either in *Miss Miller Calder's Shop* or in the *Ship's Wheel*. Sadly, these shops are no longer in existence.

The wonderfully extravagant clam shell jardinière ~ always full of flowers ~ has been the centrepiece of the front hall since The Queen Mother acquired it, along with the ebony blackamoors at the top of the staircase, from Miss Miller Calder's Shop.

Her Majesty with David Brown of the Children's Society, pictured in the front hall on his visit to the Castle of Mey.

Opposite:
Memories of gardening, beachcombing and long happy summers.

The Great Sword of Mey, a double-handed claymore, would have been wielded by the Chief of Clan Sinclair's sword bearer. It is very heavy and would have been swung in a figure of eight to devastating effect! It was possibly used at the Battle of Flodden in 1513, when William, 2nd Earl of Caithness was slain.

The highly regal hall lantern dates back to George IV's time. It is surmounted by a crown hung with tassels.

LIBRARY

In the last few years of her life
The Queen Mother used the library
as her private sitting room and study.
Here she would enjoy the
ever-changing view across
the Pentland Firth to the Orkneys.

She would often say that looking from
this window reminded her of being aboard a ship.

While in Caithness The Queen Mother enthusiastically embraced all aspects of local culture and traditions. This beautifully engraved Caithness Glass bowl was presented to her at the Mey Games in 2000.

Her Majesty receiving the glass trophy and congratulating the Castle of Mey Tug-of-War Team.

Photos: Joe Little

Before The Queen Mother began renovating the Castle, this room was the kitchen. The previous owner, Captain Imbert-Terry, had decided that the kitchen should be on this floor and had moved it from the ground floor room below. The Equerry's room next door was his dining room.

Decorated with personal memorabilia, treasured family photographs and gifts, The Queen Mother spent time here playing after-dinner games such as '*Racing Demon*' and, in later years, watching her favourite television programmes such as '*Yes Minister*', '*Fawlty Towers*' and . . .

Photo: BBC Picture Archives

During the 1960s and 1970s, guests were encouraged to liven up the after-dinner proceedings by playing the fine upright walnut piano that The Queen Mother had bought in Inverness. Ruth, Lady Fermoy, her Lady-in-Waiting, was a particularly accomplished classically-trained concert pianist.

On the top of the piano are two celebrated photographs by one of the Royal Family's favourite photographers, Norman Parkinson: Her Majesty The Queen with Princess Margaret, and The Queen with The Queen Mother.

These pictures were a present from The Queen and are signed by her and Princess Margaret.

This watercolour of the Castle was painted by Prince Charles in 1986.

The Queen Mother's wide range of interests is reflected in the choice of books on the library shelves. Here, books about Caithness are found alongside others on subjects such as gardening, natural history and horseracing.

The upper shelves contain the old Estate Ledgers from 1891 to 1948 and the Cash Book from 1915 to 1929. The Sinclair Family Bible is also here.

The Royal Society for the Protection of Birds manages reserves at Birsay Moors and Trumland on Orkney, and Forsinard north of Helmsdale in Sutherland. Hen harriers and other protected species breed on these reserves and can be seen during the summer months. This late-19th century albino hen harrier was probably bought locally.

CASTLE OF MEY
CAITHNESS

EQUERRY'S ROOM

Stationery bearing The Queen Mother's Coat of Arms lies on the desk beside Her Majesty's Bible, hymnary and psalter. It was the Equerry's responsibility to take these books to Canisbay Church every Sunday.

An excellent portrait of The Queen Mother with her much-loved corgi, *Ranger*, dominates the Equerry's room.

Painted by the artist Mara McGregor and originally hung in Clarence House, this portrait has been loaned to the Trustees by Her Majesty The Queen. It was commissioned by the Royal Warrant Holders Association for The Queen Mother's 90th birthday and was presented to her by their President, Barry Reed of the men's clothing retailer, *Austin Reed*, at the former London residence of the Strathmore family in St. James's Square. This is the only painting of The Queen Mother with the Castle of Mey in the background.

When The Queen Mother was in residence, this room was where her Equerry and Gentleman-in-Waiting would conduct her private business and correspondence.

The Castle with Aberdeen Angus by Marion Roberts, 2002.

ABERDEEN ANGUS

Renowned throughout the world for its tender and succulent meat, the superb black Aberdeen Angus has been bred in Scotland for centuries. In 1937, with her husband King George VI, Her Majesty became Joint Patron of the Aberdeen Angus Cattle Society. Over the years she developed her own prize-winning pedigree herd, with individuals gaining awards regularly at The Royal Highland Show at Edinburgh and agricultural shows in the north of Scotland. The portrait of *Castle of Mey Edwina* was presented by the Society to mark her 50 years of Patronage, her 60 years' being celebrated with an Open Day at the Castle and the presentation of the framed collection of photographs to be seen to the right of the desk in the Equerry's room. The portrait of *Castle of Mey Elscot* was the Society's present on her 100th birthday. Also displayed in the Castle are several figurines of celebrated individual cattle. In February 2003 it was announced that The Prince of Wales had taken over the Patronage of the Society from his grandmother.

The Queen Mother with an award-winning Aberdeen Angus and North Country Cheviot sheep, accompanied by her farm manager, the late Mr Donald McCarthy and his two sons, Danny and Sandy. Longoe Farm, which adjoins the Castle of Mey, is today managed jointly by Danny and Sandy and family.

1

CLOCK COLLECTION

1. FRONT HALL - (opposite page)
   This Edward VII ship's chronometer, made by Benzie of Cowes, Isle of Wight was originally installed on the first Royal Yacht *Britannia*.

2. FRONT HALL - George III mahogany bracket clock.

3. FRONT HALL - 'Act of Parliament' clock *c.*1750, made by Henlett of Bristol. These became known as 'Parliament' clocks, following the imposition of a tax on all timepieces in 1797.

4. LIBRARY - Regency rosewood clock.

5. LIBRARY - Danny's clock made by Danny Hughes, the Housekeeper's son, and given to The Queen Mother on her 100th birthday.

6. EQUERRY'S ROOM - George IV mahogany clock.

7. DRAWING ROOM - George IV rosewood clock made in Dundee *c.*1830.

8. DRAWING ROOM - Late Victorian clock set within a plinth case surmounted by a tazza.

9. DRAWING ROOM - Second Empire ormolu and bronze mantle clock.

10. DINING ROOM - Ormolu mantle clock in Louis XV style.

DRAWING ROOM

This room was re-designed in 1736 by Sir James Sinclair, 7th Laird of Mey. The Queen Mother and her guests used it every day for afternoon tea, drinks before dinner or just to read the newspapers and listen to music.

A large late 16th century Flemish wool tapestry hangs on the north wall.

For larger social occasions, the double doors between the drawing room and the Equerry's room would be opened to create a space the size of the old hall. On the doors there are beautifully ornate ceramic finger plates, bearing the cypher of the Earls of Caithness, an original feature retained by The Queen Mother.

The delightful French escritoire with secret compartments is used today to display the Castle of Mey Visitors' Book, which bears the illuminated dedication:

FOR

QUEEN ELIZABETH THE

QUEEN MOTHER

HONOURED AND BELOVED MAJESTY

this Book is made, bound, and given as a token of loyalty and gratitude

by

A. Winifred Scudamore,

Malvern - January 1955.

The Queen and her family signed the Visitors' Book having had lunch at the Castle on August 15th 1971. The photograph shows The Queen Mother steering the Scrabster lifeboat.

When The Queen Mother was in residence the peat fire in the drawing room was always burning. Much of the furniture came from antique shops nearby, and several paintings by local artists were bought in Thurso and Wick and at exhibitions held by the Society of Caithness Artists. To the left of the George III giltwood mirror above the fireplace are two bold pictures, one by Alexander Sutherland of a seascape near Wick and the other of Girnigoe Castle (above left), by his son, Alistair. The carpet was a birthday present from The Queen and is a copy of the original one made for this room. The round inlaid occasional table was made by The Queen Mother's grandson, Lord Linley.

In addition to the animals in the tapestry, you will notice the presence of a celebrated beast from Scottish folklore. The tartan 'Nessie', complete with green tam-o'shanter, was placed on top of the tapestry one night by four Irish Guards' Equerries after possibly one too many! Although an attempt was made to remove it the following morning, The Queen Mother was so amused that she instructed that it should remain there. Her Majesty's highly popular, long-serving Private Secretary, Sir Martin Gilliat, would encourage the younger guests to bring back ever more unusual souvenirs from their occasional visits to Orkney and elsewhere, as gifts for their hostess. This explains some of the Castle's more eccentric ornaments.

This birthday portrait of The Queen Mother, taken in 1963, shows much of the furniture still in place today.

DINING ROOM

This room was added in 1819 when William Burn, the renowned Scottish architect, made stylish additions to the Castle for the 12th Earl. The crenellations on the turrets date from the same period.

In 1960 the Edinburgh sculptor, Huw Lorimer, produced the carved sandstone panel bearing The Queen Mother's cypher above the south-facing window.

Arguably the most opulent interior in the Castle, this room contains many reminders of The Queen Mother's royal status: treasured pictures, works of art, gifts and trophies all combine to create a wonderfully elegant yet informal atmosphere.

On the east wall is the fabulous tapestry of her Royal Coat of Arms, designed by Stephen Goodan RA and woven by R. Cruickshank, R.B. Gordon and J. Luttit at the Ducat Studios in Edinburgh in 1950.

At the opposite end of the room is the equally beautiful bronze fire-back by the late Lord Charteris, a talented artist and sculptor, and The Queen's longest serving Private Secretary. He not only designed it, beating out the images in copper on the reverse, but also carried out all the casting work himself. This much treasured piece depicts The Queen Mother's cypher and the Royal Yacht *Britannia* amongst local flora and fauna.

The naïve picture above the fireplace was painted by R.I. Gray in 1884 and probably commemorates a visit by the Prince and Princess of Wales a few years earlier. Prophetically it shows a herd of Aberdeen Angus cattle grazing near the Castle with the Royal Yacht of the day anchored offshore. The Queen Mother was delighted to buy the painting when it was offered to her by the executors of the estate of a lady from Wick.

Either side of the fireplace are two oil paintings by HRH Prince Philip. This is a view of the Castle from the East Garden.

Edward, Prince of Wales, later King Edward VII, is depicted in this decorative tapestry firescreen. It was presented to Her Majesty by her long-serving Lady-in-Waiting, Lady Victoria Wemyss. The image is taken from a painting by Winterhalter.

Displayed on the side-table is the Sinclair Punch Bowl which was given to Lord Berriedale, later 15th Earl of Caithness, by tenants and friends of the estate on the occasion of his 21st birthday on 30th November 1879. It portrays the Castle and other local scenes including views of Canisbay Church, Huna Harbour, and John o'Groats. Also displayed is part of a Derby dessert service and a ceremonial sword. The latter was presented to The Queen Mother on the occasion of her 100th birthday by the Regiments and Corps of which she was Colonel-in-Chief.

BUTLER'S PANTRY & KITCHEN

This royal kitchen was the favourite of Head Chef, Michael Sealey
who worked for The Queen Mother for almost 50 years
until her Household was disbanded in April 2002.

He loved to harvest the fruit and vegetables in the working
garden and appreciated the views beyond to Dunnet Head (opposite),
the most northerly point of mainland Britain,
and across the Pentland Firth to the Orkney Isles.

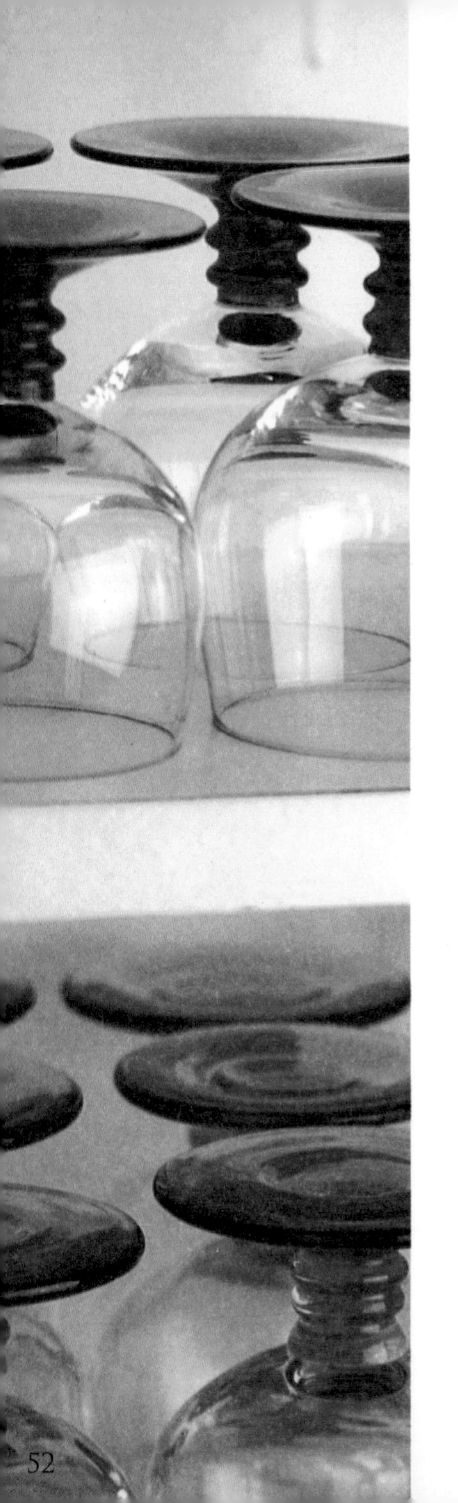

BUTLER'S PANTRY

To see this remarkable little room is to step back in time to the late 1950s and early 1960s.
The period fixtures and fittings evoke memories of Mrs Beaton and Fanny Cradock rather than Gary Rhodes and Jamie Oliver!

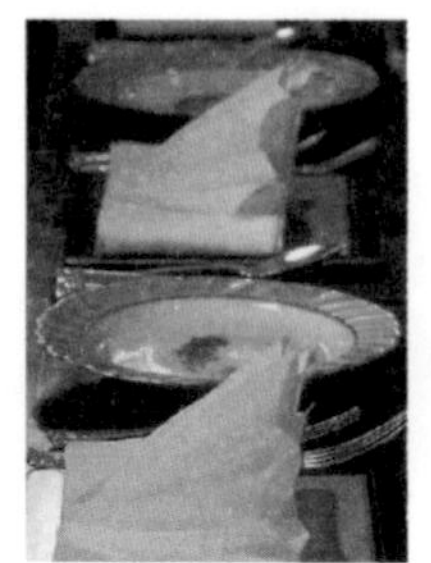

By adding this room to house all the plates, glassware and cutlery, The Queen Mother found it much easier to entertain guests in the dining room next door.

The Duty Page would polish silver here during the day and in the evening, when dinner was in progress, the footmen would keep the plates and food warm in the old electric oven.

The food-lift or dumbwaiter, installed to take everything up and down to the kitchen below, was hand-operated. However, the pages and footmen preferred to go up and down the steep stairs rather than listen to the excruciating sounds that emanated from it when it was in use. Because meals could be spoiled by the noise, the lift was rarely used but there were plans to electrify it and make it silent.

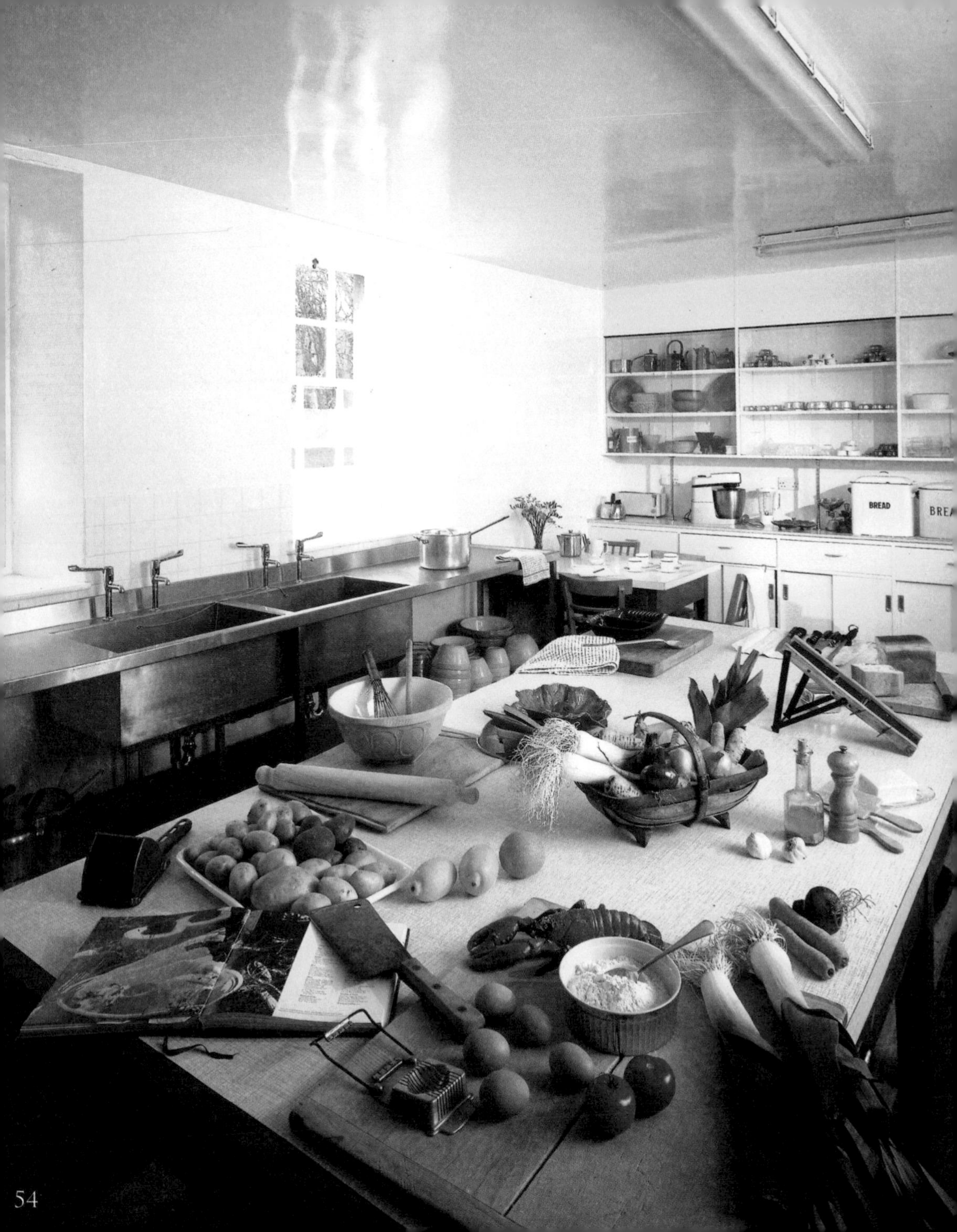
BREAD
BREA

KITCHEN

Head Chef, Michael Sealey, greatly enjoyed catering for The Queen Mother in the Castle kitchen.

On good days the sun spills in through the south-facing windows which were nearly always left open when cooking was in progress. In contrast to some other royal kitchens, this one has a spendid view and is exceptionally airy and light.

Each Christmas the children from the local school are presented with a cake made by the Castle's Housekeeper and staff. This tradition was started by The Queen Mother and is continued today by The Prince of Wales.

Preserved with great care since its installation in the 1960s, the classic 'Frigidaire' refrigerator still works perfectly today.

GARDENS

Severe winds in this remote part of the country are able to pluck a cabbage from the bleak earth and fling it 60 feet. Without the 15-foot high 'Great Wall of Mey', this working garden, comprising around two acres, would not enjoy protection from the fierce gales and sea spray that blow in from the Pentland Firth.

The Queen Mother loved sitting on the little bench in the Shell Garden (bottom left opposite).

August 1999. The Queen Mother's love of colour in furniture and fashion also found its way into the flowers of the herbaceous borders and the old-fashioned shrub roses in the Shell Garden.

Gardens and gardening were in Her Majesty's blood. Her mother, the Countess of Strathmore and Kinghorne, was a renowned expert. The family homes in which The Queen Mother grew up, Glamis Castle in Scotland and St. Paul's Walden Bury in Hertfordshire, both have outstanding gardens. The Countess created the stunning Italian Garden at Glamis.

The Italian Garden, Glamis.

Copyright: RCAHMS

The Queen Mother's love of gardening started when, as Duchess of York, she took on the garden at Royal Lodge in Windsor Great Park in 1931. After World War II, several other royal houses benefited from her horticultural skills and enthusiasm. As Queen she planted ornamental trees and shrubs at Buckingham Palace and she created Sandringham's formal garden and large areas of rhododendrons, camellias and magnolias. Despite many difficulties and set-backs, The Queen Mother's experienced green fingers ensured that the garden at the Castle of Mey prospered. She even managed to nurture her favourite old rose, Albertine, into abundance behind an intricate network of 6-foot high hedges of privet, currant and elder. The garden is full of marigolds, pansies, dahlias, primulas and nasturtiums; sweet peas, old-fashioned shrub roses and climbers being the highlights of the Shell Garden. The greenhouse displays marigolds, begonias and lobelias, amongst other varieties of plants. This romantic and unique garden is a reminder that, however daunting the weather, it is possible to create and maintain a successful garden. The Castle kitchen benefited from the wide variety of fruit and vegetables grown here, all chosen for their resistance to wind and sea spray. Raspberries, strawberries, gooseberries, apples, currants, potatoes, peas, beans, carrots, turnips, onions and leeks all thrive here and, for some unknown reason, the exotic artichoke does extremely well too! Although The Queen Mother contributed greatly to many royal gardens, it is the Castle of Mey's that is more ***hers*** than any other. With much dedication over several decades, she transformed what was a daunting and inhospitable spot into the stunning garden seen today, designed to be at its peak when she visited in August.

It is perhaps no coincidence that her grandson, Prince Charles, is today one of our most celebrated royal gardeners. He is helping the Trustees to extend the growing season - no easy task this far north. The changes, planned by well known garden designers Julian and Isabel Bannerman, are being generously paid for by a fund set up by Mr. Peter Fowler, the proprietor of North of Scotland Newspapers. *The John O'Groat Journal*, which The Queen Mother enjoyed receiving throughout the year, is one of his publications.

CANISBAY CHURCH

Since her first attendance in April 1959, The Queen Mother became a regular worshipper at this ancient pre-Reformation kirk, the most northerly place of worship on the Scottish mainland. Like the Earls of Caithness before her, she occupied the Castle Pew in the north transept. The Praise Board in the church was presented by her in 1976.

April 1959.
The Queen Mother bids farewell to the Rev. George Bell, after attending the service in Canisbay Church for the first time.

She was to worship here for a further 42 years whatever the weather.

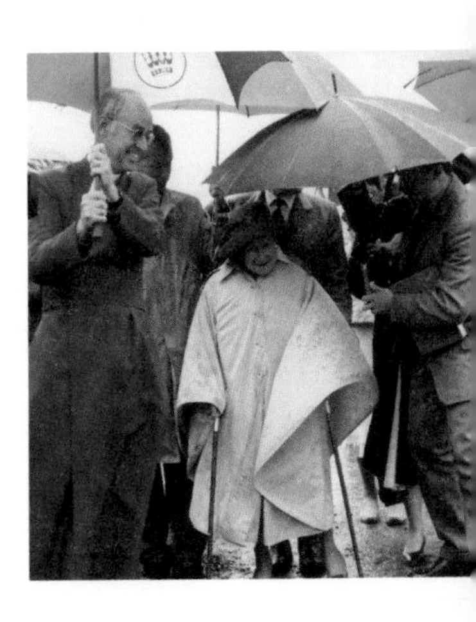

In the mind of the general public John o'Groats has for many years been most closely associated with Land's End. Thousands of long distance walkers and cyclists have made the 874-mile trek from Cornwall to Caithness and vice versa in aid of charity. The name, John o'Groats, originated in the 16th century when a certain Jan de Groat was granted a licence to operate a ferry between the mainland and the Orkney Islands for the fee of a single groat. Jan de Groat died on 13th April 1568 and was buried here in the church. His engraved tombstone, originally situated under the church floor, can be seen today in the vestibule. Behind iron railings on the north side of the church is the family vault of the Sinclairs of Mey. Here a stone bearing the initial 'S' marks the grave of Lady Fanny Sinclair, only daughter of the 14th Earl of Caithness. Tragically, both she and, in 1889, her brother, the 15th Earl, died young and unmarried, bringing that line of the Earls of Caithness to an end.

The highlight of a gruelling sponsored cycle ride from Land's End to John o'Groats for a priest and one of his parishioners, is to meet The Queen Mother outside the church on Sunday morning.

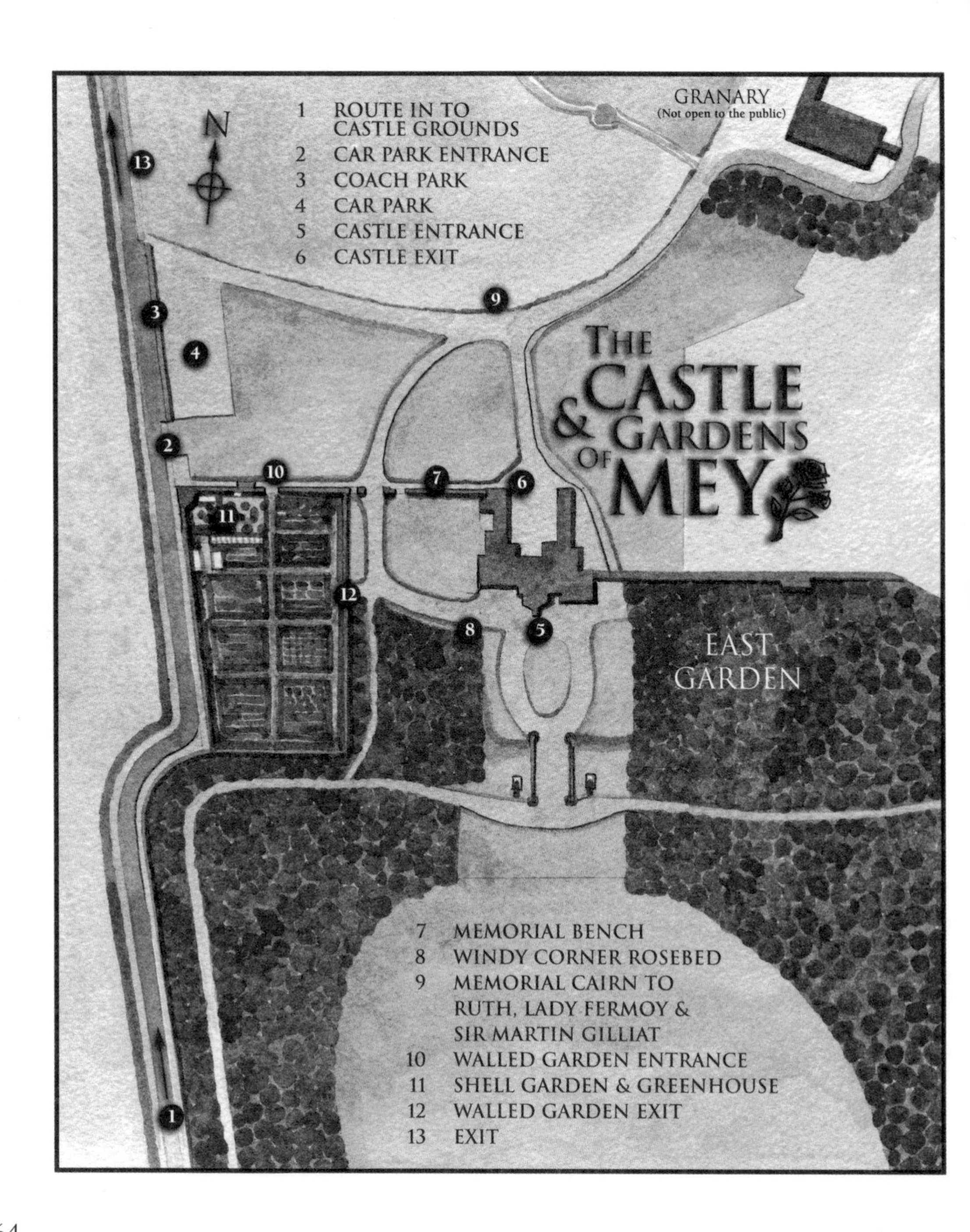
1 ROUTE IN TO CASTLE GROUNDS
2 CAR PARK ENTRANCE
3 COACH PARK
4 CAR PARK
5 CASTLE ENTRANCE
6 CASTLE EXIT
N
GRANARY
(Not open to the public)
THE CASTLE & GARDENS OF MEY
EAST GARDEN
7 MEMORIAL BENCH
8 WINDY CORNER ROSEBED
9 MEMORIAL CAIRN TO RUTH, LADY FERMOY & SIR MARTIN GILLIAT
10 WALLED GARDEN ENTRANCE
11 SHELL GARDEN & GREENHOUSE
12 WALLED GARDEN EXIT
13 EXIT

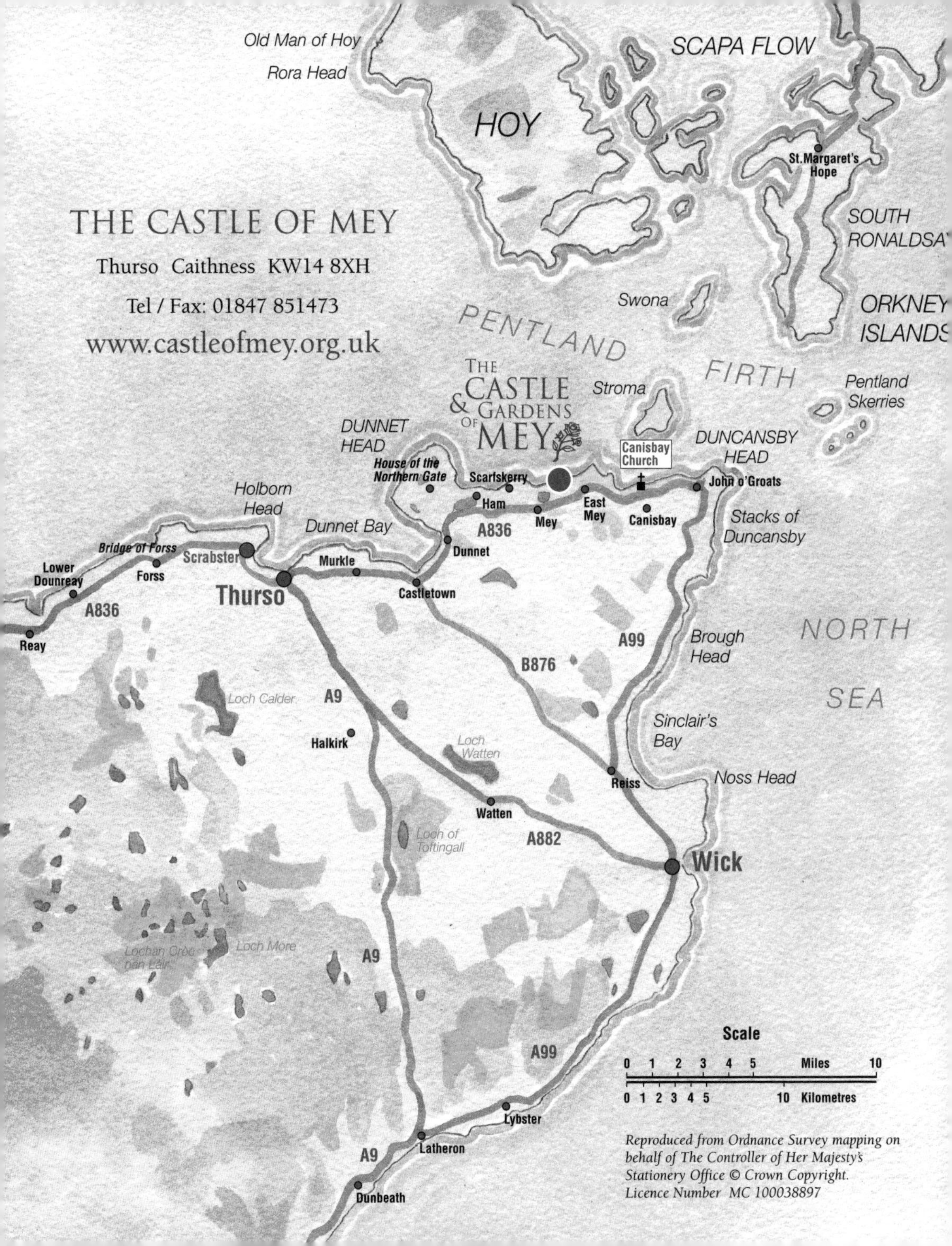

Old Man of Hoy
Rora Head
SCAPA FLOW
HOY
St.Margaret's Hope
SOUTH RONALDSA
ORKNEY ISLANDS
THE CASTLE OF MEY
Thurso Caithness KW14 8XH
Tel / Fax: 01847 851473
www.castleofmey.org.uk
Swona
PENTLAND
FIRTH
THE CASTLE & GARDENS OF MEY
Stroma
Pentland Skerries
DUNNET HEAD
House of the Northern Gate
Scarfskerry
Canisbay Church
DUNCANSBY HEAD
John o'Groats
Ham
Mey
East Mey
Canisbay
Holborn Head
Dunnet Bay
A836
Stacks of Duncansby
Bridge of Forss
Scrabster
Dunnet
Lower Dounreay
Forss
Murkle
Thurso
Castletown
A836
Reay
NORTH
A99
Brough Head
B876
Loch Calder
A9
SEA
Sinclair's Bay
Halkirk
Loch Watten
Reiss
Noss Head
Watten
Loch of Toftingall
A882
Wick
Lochan Cree nan Lair
Loch More
A9
Scale
A99
0 1 2 3 4 5 Miles 10
0 1 2 3 4 5 10 Kilometres
Lybster
Latheron
A9
Dunbeath

The Castle & Gardens of Mey

Written & Designed by Nick McCann
Interior Photography primarily by Peter Smith,
with additional pictures by John Adams - courtesy of North of Scotland Newspapers,
BBC Picture Archives, Joe Little, Nick McCann, J. McDonald Photographers, Wick,
Royal Commission on the Ancient and Historical Monuments of Scotland and
Christopher Simon Sykes at The Interior Archive.

The author and publishers would like to thank the following for their assistance and contributions to this project: Clive Richards and his splendid book *The Queen Mother and Family at home in Caithness*, Grant Napier - Head Gardener of the Castle of Mey for his notes on the Garden, James Murray - Trust Administrator, Barbara Hiddlestone - Trust Historian and Archivist, for her research material and text on the Castle's history and architecture, and Dr. Iain Macnee - Minister of Canisbay Church.

Published and produced by Heritage House Group Ltd.,
Heritage House, Lodge Lane, Derby DE1 3HE Tel: 01332 347087 Fax: 01332 290688
e.mail: publications@hhgroup.co.uk

Printed in Great Britain